Financing Transitions:
Managing Capital
and Liquidity
in the Family Business

François M. de Visscher,
Craig E. Aronoff, Ph.D.
and John L. Ward, Ph.D.

Family Business Leadership Series, No.7

Family Enterprise Publishers
P.O. Box 4356
Marietta, GA 30061-4356
800-551-0633
www.efamilybusiness.com

ISSN: 1071-5010
ISBN: 0-9651011-7-7
© 1995
Fourth printing

Family Business Leadership Series

We believe that family businesses are special, not only to the families that own and manage them but also to our society and to the private enterprise system. Having worked and interacted with hundreds of family enterprises in the past twenty years, we offer the insights of that experience and the collected wisdom of the world's best and most successful family firms.

This volume is a part of a series offering practical guidance for family businesses seeking to manage the special challenges and opportunities confronting them.

To order additional copies, contact:
Family Enterprise Publishers
1220-B Kennestone Circle
Marietta, Georgia 30066
Tel: 800-551-0633
Web Site: www.efamilybusiness.com

Quantity discounts are available.

Other volumes in the series include:

Contents

Tables and Exhibits

I. *Introduction*

■

"Meet the environment's needs today in a way that doesn't compromise the opportunity for future generations to do the same."
　　　　　　　　　　—Sam Johnson, Chairman, S.C. Johnson & Sons

■

If a family business is to endure and provide the maximum potential opportunity for future generations, planning to provide adequate liquidity for shareholders and capital for the business is crucial. Yet family businesses may face a real dilemma when they wrestle with these issues. As pressures mount, many believe they have only limited options: Do without, sell out or go public.

The good news is that a growing number of successful family businesses are thriving through multiple generations of family ownership, providing models for other families. More than a decade of "financial engineering" on Wall Street has multiplied the tools at families' disposal to help them finance the kinds of transitions in management, ownership and strategy that have destroyed family businesses in the past. Rather than facing questions of selling out or going public, many family businesses now find the central issue is maintaining control over decisionmaking to permit wise, well-timed choices about the many alternatives available to them.

This booklet is a guide to anticipating and managing capital and liquidity needs in your business. Its mission is to help you keep control over decisionmaking, and to keep family control of the business. It presents tools to manage business capital and shareholder liquidity needs, including for the first time the important concept of the "Family Effect" and a new formula for gauging shareholders' expected rate of return. And it describes in detail an array of up-to-date financial solutions for providing liquidity and capital to the family business.

Specifically, the next section of the booklet, "How Transitions Can Erode Family Control," shows how predictable transitions common among family businesses can erupt into financial crises. Section III, "Managing Your Liquidity Needs," lays a framework for liquidity planning, illustrating the hazards of the "downward liquidity spiral"

1

that is all too common among family businesses and offering tips on how to avoid it. Section IV, "Managing Your Cost of Capital," lays out the unique components of the cost of capital in the family business and offers tips on maintaining the family business' core competitive advantage—"patient capital." Section V, "To Sell or Not To Sell," offers a brief discussion of the pros and cons of selling out. Finally, Section VI, "Financial Solutions: Maintaining Family Control Through the Generations," describes nearly two dozen up-to-date financial solutions that can help you meet capital and liquidity needs in your business.

In sum, the book aims to give the business owner the financial tools and understanding needed to provide future generations the fullest possible opportunity to enjoy the unique benefits of business ownership. This includes not only the chance to create wealth and rewarding careers for family members, but the opportunity to convey to the world at large the family pride, cohesiveness and shared goals and values that are manifested by a healthy family business.

II. *How Transitions Can Erode Family Control*

Family businesses usually start out small. Sufficient funding is typically among the challenges they face. As the business matures, the family looks forward to the business' growth to provide solutions to many of the financial issues it faces — only to find that business success and growth create new and more complicated financial matters to confront them. Money to finance growth, to meet competitive challenges, to provide personal security, to reward ownership, to provide for the needs of an ever-growing family, to develop the business organization, to pay estate taxes — it's no wonder that many family businesses choose to stay small. But small or large, especially when the time comes for transitions between generations, family businesses face daunting decisions.

Patient Capital. One of the key competitive advantages of family businesses wrestling with these decisions is "patient capital." **Patient capital is equity provided by family business founders or successors who are willing to balance the current return on their business investment with the merits of a well-crafted long-term strategy and continuation of the family tradition and heritage**. Such investors assume that attaining solid long-term growth is worth foregoing maximum short-term gains. Their attitude gives a business tremendous leverage to build market share and compete effectively at relatively lower cost of capital than widely-held or publicly-traded companies.

In the lore of North American business, patient capital has traditionally been seen as an advantage enjoyed by somebody else— Japanese businesses, for instance, whose owners are culturally attuned to taking the long view. More recently, big investors on Wall Street are trying to foster their own version of patient capital with a move toward "relationship investing"—a willingness by shareholders to shift their focus away from quarter-to-quarter profit gains toward forging a commitment to a company, a trend trumpeted by *Business Week* as "a provocative new investment idea." (Judith H. Dobrzynski, March 15, 1993, p. 68.)

In fact, **few companies can match the family business' potential for investor cohesiveness and commitment**. A tight-knit, hard-working base of family shareholders is united not only by family ties, but by shared values, common goals and a willingness to work hard together to achieve them.

How Transitions Can Wipe Out Patient Capital. Yet family businesses continue to expire at an alarming rate. Of 200 successful manufacturers in existence in 1924, only 20 percent survived as independent companies 60 years later, and only 13 percent were still owned by the same family (Ward, 1987). Even among those where family ownership endured, only three percent grew significantly. The rest either failed to grow or declined.

Many family businesses die because capital or liquidity problems prevent them from surviving generational, strategic or ownership transitions. The business may lack capital to grow and compete or to meet a new generation of shareholders' demands for current income. In early generation family businesses, a key shareholder's death may give rise to overwhelming estate tax demands. A shareholder's personal financial problems may create a need to sell a large block of stock. Or the business may need cash for a critical strategic move just as shareholders' demand for current return increases. For later generation family businesses, the business may not provide the necessary return or inspire the cohesiveness and commitment required to keep shareholders' patient capital intact. These problems do not develop overnight. They often simmer unnoticed for years before flaring into crises that rob controlling owners of constructive alternatives. **In a flash of financial alchemy, patient capital becomes demanding capital, and the family business is suddenly at risk**.

Many of these crises can be planned for and even avoided altogether. Typically they arise out of predictable transitions faced by most family businesses. These transitions usually fall into one of three categories.

Generational Transitions

Early in his career, the great center fielder Willie Mays liked to play close to the infield hoping to nail baserunners from the outfield. The result: his most spectacular catches, glove outstretched over his shoulder, came as he raced at top speed toward the center-field wall — a risky approach necessitated by his aggressive fielding. As Mays aged, he played deeper and deeper in the outfield. Asked about his retreat, he explained, "I'm getting too old to outrun my mistakes."

Like Willie Mays, many family business founders or senior generation family members get more conservative as they grow older. The math is simple: They have fewer years left to correct missteps. They may try even harder to control the course of the business, clamping down on details and avoiding risk. **As the years wear on, their own personal security in retirement looms larger as a financial concern, intensifying their tendency to conservatism.**

4

This natural evolution in senior family members' goals and attitudes can clash head-on with an opposite tendency: the desire of the successor generation to take risks and bring about change. Younger managers may feel the business isn't changing fast enough to keep up with the world around them. Typically in their thirties and influenced by having grown up in relative ease and affluence, successors are often willing to take risks and grow the business. They want control of business strategy, often embracing the "continuous improvement" advocated by business schools — in direct opposition to their elders' plea, "If it ain't broke, don't fix it." Successors may be eager to invest in new strategies or markets, expanding their base of operation to match the energy and sense of promise they feel. They also may be eager to upgrade their living standard from that of the more frugal senior generation members.

While the dilemma of growth vs. cash conservation is not foreign to most businesses' strategic planning process, it poses a particular difficulty in a family business environment, where owners must reconcile conflicting demands for the same pile of money. The successor generation wants to risk business capital on grand long-term strategies. The older generation hopes to conserve cash for security and avoid strategies that seem risky. The two sides have difficulty pursuing common goals because their top priorities— growing the business vs. providing financial security — naturally conflict. In more mature multigenerational family businesses, the same intergenerational conflict may arise between shareholders who seek long-term returns and those who desire current income.

The family may need to raise additional capital to reduce the dependence of the younger generation on the older generation by buying out or even providing liquidity opportunities for some shareholders. That's how the transition from one generation of family owners to the next becomes a financing issue. Without additional capital, these normal intergenerational conflicts may erupt into crises that may ultimately cripple or end family control over the business.

Strategic Transitions

Each new generation must revitalize family business strategy.

And today, a strategic renewal every 25 years or so may not even be frequent enough. Accelerating business change, intensifying international competition and shortened product life cycles are forcing successful businesses in many industries into a mode of almost constant strategic renewal. **In the future, each generation of family-business**

5

managers may have to revitalize strategy several times. Strategic planning becomes a perpetual discipline. Innovation becomes a continual pattern. Highly professional management becomes the norm.

Continually reinvesting in the business becomes a necessity to maintain competitiveness in the market and, ultimately, shareholder value. The family business of the future must be able to marshal the necessary capital to make well-timed acquisitions, expand into new markets, hire new people, develop new products or buy new equipment. **Its shareholders must be cohesive, motivated and committed enough to take risks and build the business for the future — a kind of unity we call "the Family Effect" and describe in detail later in this book.**

Without this kind of shareholder commitment and flexibility, many business-owning families will fail to revitalize strategy, allowing opportunities to slip away and ultimately diminishing shareholder value or even family control.

Ownership Transitions

Ownership transitions create the most familiar yet least foreseeable kinds of liquidity crises in family business. A controlling shareholder dies and estate-tax liabilities force the sale of the business. One of two partners in the business dies and the other must buy out the surviving spouse. A key employee who owns stock retires and the stock must be redeemed. In multigenerational family businesses, younger generation shareholders may lose their cohesiveness and sense of commitment to the business and may demand higher current return on their capital.

Ownership transitions create external and internal liquidity demands — external estate tax liabilities, and internal shareholder liquidity demands. Ownership transitions spread capital among a much larger base of shareholders, diluting control in the shareholder base. This in turn may reduce family members' commitment and cohesiveness and create a demand for higher current return.

As shown in Table 1, the nature of family ownership and the expectations family shareholders have of the business change substantially from generation to generation. Like the gradual, centuries-long shifts in the earth's surface that ultimately create volcanos, these evolutionary changes in family ownership must be addressed lest they erupt into a liquidity crisis that destroys the business.

6

Table 1: _____

EVOLUTION OF FAMILY CONTROL NEEDS			
Generation	**First Generation: Owner/Manager** **Stage I**	**Second Generation: Sibling/Partnership** **Stage II**	**Third Generation: Cousin/Collaborative** **Stage III**
Ownership Structure	Concentrated Ownership Among Founder or Founders	Emergence of Inactive Shareholders	Advent of Minority Shareholder Class; Transition from Family Ownership to Family Control
Liquidity Sources	Owner's Compensation	Dividends & Limited Internal Redemptions	Dividends, Internal Redemptions and Outside Capital
Capital Sources	Primarily Business Cash Flow	Business Cash Flow & Some External Debt or Equity Financing	Capital Needs of the Business Far Exceed the Means of the Family, Requiring a Search for Outside Capital.
Causes of Financial Conflict	Cash Flow Allocation Between Business and Personal Use	Dividends to All Holders Vs. Salary and Benefits to Active Shareholders	Tension Between Goals of Business Growth vs. Shareholder Desire for Current Return Differences Over Adequate Return on Equity

Let's take a closer look at these generation-by-generation changes.

First Generation — Owner/Manager Stage: Concentrated Ownership. The founder-generation family business provides a backdrop against which the advantages and disadvantages of later generations of family ownership can be seen. In this founding or entrepreneurial stage, family control is at its firmest, most intense and most forceful, placing relatively few demands on the business and instead feeding it with entrepreneurial energy and drive. Ownership typically is concentrated in the hands of one or two shareholders who are committed to agreed-upon goals. Shareholder liquidity needs are met by the owner's salary, benefits and perks. Financial decisions are driven by tax planning and cash flow allocation. Business capital needs are met by cash flow that is plowed back into the business. The primary source of conflict by shareholders, if any, is how cash flow from the business will be used. A shareholder might experience an unforeseen need for cash that could raise questions about draining capital from the business. But generally, this stage is one of relative cohesiveness in the face of the challenges of building a business.

Second Generation — Sibling/Partnership Stage: Birth of the Inactive Shareholder. The goals and expectations of family business shareholders often begin to diverge as early as the second generation, quenching the energizing effect of cohesive family ownership. As stock passes to heirs of the entrepreneur(s), some may not wish to be active in the business, either by choice or not. If inactive shareholders are neglected or uninformed about the business or feel "shut out," unappreciated, exploited or needy, their inactive status creates the potential for two kinds of conflict over capital and liquidity. First, they may grow resentful of those who are working in the business and receiving salary, perks, recognition and so on. They easily become suspicious that active shareholders are exploiting the business by draining too much cash for their own compensation or their own pet management projects. Second, **if inactive holders feel dividends are their only reward for ownership, they may begin focusing on current income at the expense of long-term business growth**. A pattern may be set of inactive holders pressing for dividend increases and greater shareholder liquidity, regardless of the impact on the business. This is the seed of a classic conflict that has destroyed many family businesses.

Third Generation — Cousin/Collaborative Stage: Resolving Diverse Family Interests. The conflicts between active and inactive shareholders may take center stage in latter generations of family ownership as shareholder factions become more outspoken. Unless steps have been taken to fortify the family's commitment to the business and family ownership, shareholders' financial goals diverge even more at this stage. Shareholder factions are larger and more diverse, and may be more conscious of their power. Branches of the family may disagree over an array of issues, not the least of which are how to use cash and how to harness the business' economic power. These conflicts are made even more difficult by the fact that most businesses outgrow the financial means of the owning family by this stage. Additional capital must be raised outside the business if it is to grow and thrive.

This may imply that the family may give up total control of the business in order to endure as a family-controlled enterprise. This does not necessarily mean going public. It may mean looking outside the family for partners to provide equity capital. It may mean creating capital through strategic means such as business alliances, joint ventures or disposing of assets, as discussed later in this booklet.

Also, the family's role in the business often undergoes a significant evolution by this stage. The necessity of professional management may reduce family involvement in day-to-day management. The empowerment of outside management changes the family's role in the control structure of the business in a way not encountered before.

The advent of a new empowered management structure also may heighten conflicts between active and inactive shareholders. Inactive holders may focus even more intensely on short-term returns, hindering attempts by active holders and management to pursue riskier long-term strategies. All of these factors can drive the family to give up an equity stake in the company and begin to focus more on providing all owners, active family, inactive family or even outside equity holders, a fair return on capital.

How Two Families Met the Challenge. Let's take a look at how two third-generation, family-owned companies managed these transitions. The two businesses began early in this century with much in common, including a strong first generation of family owners and tremendous growth potential. But the decisions each family made about how to manage liquidity and capital needs led to completely different outcomes. One of the businesses continues to grow and thrive, providing opportunity for a fourth generation of family owners and multiplying wealth for shareholders. The other was unable to meet the strategic demands of its markets or the liquidity demands of its shareholders, leaving the family with no choice but to sell out. The cases are real but their names have been disguised.

Case One: Donovan's Debt Trap

The founder of this East Coast-based textile-machine manufacturer started the business shortly after the turn of the century. His two sons and daughter inherited his stock in equal stakes, though only the sons were active in the business.

Though the founder was a visionary in setting business strategy, he failed to plan for continuing family ownership and planted the seeds of a liquidity crisis that ultimately forced the business' sale. When the daughter, feeling somewhat disenfranchised, needed liquidity and asked to redeem her shares, the sons took on debt to buy her out. Later, one of the sons ran into marital problems and began to drain cash through

9

consulting and employment contracts. Then, the textile industry moved south, forcing the company to redirect itself into different industries amid all the problems with shareholders.

By the time the first son died and estate taxes came due, the founder's descendants had no means to pay. Their only option was to sell.

Case Two: The Growth of the Eagle Co.

This Southwestern food-processing concern was started in 1920 by a founder who had not only strategic vision, but an understanding of future capital and liquidity issues the business would face.

This founder also had two sons and a daughter. But while he was still active in the business he carefully arranged with the help of excellent attorneys, shareholder liquidity programs to redeem stock through installment purchases financed by case flow. This avoided the need to finance lump-sum buyouts with debt. When his daughter later decided to redeem her shares, the program helped keep the company on solid financial footing. The founder also started early to educate shareholders by communicating about dividend policy.

Training of the younger generation and a free flow of information to all family members became a hallmark of the business. By the third generation, the family conducted Saturday morning seminars for the seven members of the successor generation. "Senior" or "junior" boards of directors were formed to encourage family members to learn about and be involved in the business. Meanwhile, the company grew rapidly, topping $1 billion in annual sales and generating plenty of excess cash. Today, prospects are good for the four members of the third generation who are active in the business, and for inactive shareholders as well.

Alike but Profoundly Different. These two family businesses would seem to a casual observer to have much in common:

■ founded about the same time;
■ strong first generation;
■ weak second generation;
■ adequate growth potential;
■ liquidity demands from shareholders;
■ internal cash flow sufficient to meet the business' capital needs.

But the radical difference in the way the two businesses managed and met liquidity demands from shareholders was enough to set each on a path toward opposite destinies:

- One used cash flow to redeem shares, the other used debt;
- One educated inactive shareholders, the other merely indulged them;
- One kept shareholders informed about the business and the basis for dividend policy, the other did not;
- One smoothed ownership transitions through training members of the younger generation, the other failed to prepare them at all;
- One deliberately maintained a steady flow of information to shareholders, the other did not.
- Most important, the founder of one company had the foresight to plan to manage a variety of issues that would affect future capital and liquidity, while the other did not.

In the next section of this book, we will discuss some important principles and patterns that form the foundation of this kind of capital and liquidity planning in the family business.

III. *Managing Your Liquidity Needs*

■

—"You can never plan the future by the past."
—Edmund Burke, 1791

■

At the root of transitional crises of the kind that forced the sale of the Donovan family business is a lack of capital and liquidity planning. **Availing themselves of modern management techniques, most family businesses commit to some strategic planning to meet business capital needs. But few incorporate in their planning the need to meet shareholder liquidity demands**.

The Donovan company failed to plan for shareholder liquidity and made crucial mistakes as a result. It took on ill-advised debt to buy out a shareholder, rather than preparing shareholders to accept more gradual, realistic solutions to liquidity problems. It also failed to place reasonable constraints on the liquidity demands of a second shareholder. It failed to plan for adequate capital to meet the changing imperatives of its industry. And it failed to anticipate a liquidity crisis upon the death of the oldest shareholder, when estate-tax demands dealt a final, killing blow to family control of the business.

All of these problems might have been eased or avoided with careful planning. This need for **"TLC"— to think about liquidity and capital** — begins early, typically as early as the transition from first to second generation family ownership. **Capital and liquidity are particularly tough issues as the family business matures, because they so often conflict**. The business needs capital to thrive and grow. Shareholders want or need the same cash to meet their personal goals.

This natural conflict is forced into the open when a cash shortage develops. The necessary tradeoffs often put a spotlight on long-term goals. Discussion of an acquisition plan might raise the issue, "We can't take that risk because we're a family business. Everybody is counting on us for dividends." Or the need to buy out a partner's widow might force the business owner to postpone equipment purchases or diversification plans.

The conflict is worsened by the fact that outside equity capital for a

13

family business is typically more costly than for large, publicly-traded companies. Some family business owners meet this challenge by pursuing conservative growth plans which require less outside financing. While this strategy works for some, it may pose long-term risks of weakening the business or rendering it unable to support the family. Other family businesses hold down capital needs by asking successor generations to make some of the same sacrifices entrepreneurs made in the startup stages of a business, forcing on successors some extremely difficult decisions.

The Most Important Objective. Amid these conflicting forces, **it is crucial for the business owner to maintain control over the decisionmaking process** so that all of these complexities can be weighed and a full range of options considered. To accomplish this, a delicate balance must be preserved between the capital needs of the business and the liquidity needs of the family. This balance is not unlike that achieved by a tightrope walker or a running back zigzagging through a line of opposing blockers. A graphic illustration of this balance is contained in Exhibit 1, "The Family Business Triangle."

EXHIBIT 1

The Family Business Triangle

Balancing three needs in a family business system

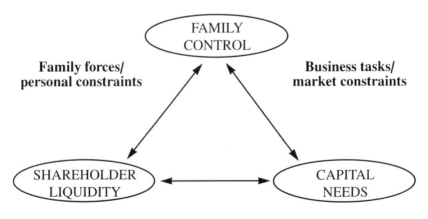

FAMILY CONTROL

Family forces/ personal constraints

Business tasks/ market constraints

SHAREHOLDER LIQUIDITY

CAPITAL NEEDS

™de Visscher & Company

The triangle portrays the tension intrinsic to the financial life of a family business as it passes from generation to generation. If family control is to be sustained at the top of the triangle, equilibrium between shareholder liquidity and the capital needs of the business must be achieved at its base.

When liquidity and capital needs drift apart for any reason, equilibrium is lost. Any tendency of family business shareholders to expand their "harvest" of the business' assets can pull the left base of the triangle out of position and undermine family control. In countless family businesses that have failed or fallen apart, the same pattern prevails: Dividends per share go up, while earnings per share spiral downward. Diverging liquidity and capital needs pull the triangle apart and family control collapses. (See Exhibit 2.)

EXHIBIT 2 ▄▄▄▄▄▄▄▄▄▄▄▄▄▄▄▄▄▄▄▄▄▄▄▄▄▄▄▄▄▄▄▄▄▄▄▄

The Compressed Triangle

When the liquidity and capital needs drift apart, control is lost

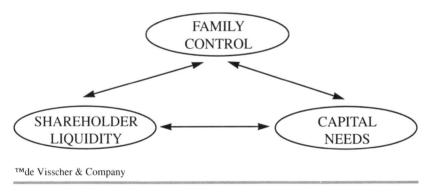

™de Visscher & Company

This delicate balance is in many ways unique to the family business. In a public company, a shareholder's decision to buy or sell stock has no bearing on either capital available to the business or control of the business. The deep, liquid public equity markets mediate both functions. But in a family business, cash is often short from the start. Any decision by a shareholder to sell stock or otherwise demand a high current return affects both of the other two points of the triangle. Similarly, any decision by a public company to plow capital back into the business usually has little direct impact on shareholder liquidity. But channelling family business cash into operations or acquisitions can easily affect both family control and shareholder liquidity. None of the three needs can undergo a change without altering the financial equilibrium of the entire system.

Red Flags in Capital and Liquidity Planning. What are some signals that shareholder liquidity needs may diverge from business capital needs?

As shown in Table 2, some liquidity needs are immediate — the need to pay estate taxes or respond to a shareholder's divorce, for instance. Other forces that can compress the family business triangle are evolutionary. Few family businesses anticipate the gradual changes in family members' attitudes, lifestyle expenses or personal investment goals that can require cash from the business.

A variety of family factors can spark liquidity demands. If family

Table 2: _____

FACTORS THAT TEND TO INCREASE FAMILY BUSINESS SHAREHOLDER DEMANDS FOR LIQUIDITY

Occasional Factors
- Death of a shareholder
- Divorce of a shareholder
- Personal financial bankruptcy
- Business ventures
- Other personal financial crises

Family Factors
- Weakening of family cohesiveness and commitment
- Limited recognition of inactive shareholders to business success
- Conflicts between active and inactive shareholders
- Heavy dependency by shareholders on income from the business
- Heavy family responsibilities among shareholders
- Concentration of shareholders in the same age groups

Financial Factors
- Shareholder disappointment in current returns
- Lack of shareholder access to appreciation
- Lackluster total return on equity (dividends plus appreciation)
- Shareholder need to diversify investment
- Reinvestment opportunities elsewhere for shareholders to multiply wealth

members are close in age to each other, for instance, their cash demands are more likely to converge. Business capital can be drained when several family members face college costs or other large expenditures. Obviously, shareholders who lack adequate income from other sources, who are unable to save money, or who have a relatively large number of children are more likely, other things being equal, to demand cash from the business. And **shareholders who lack emotional attachment to the family or whose family relationships are troubled also are more likely to pressure the business for cash**.

Shareholders' investment plans and desires also play a role. If shareholders are disappointed in the business' performance or lack access to appreciation in its value, they may press for greater liquidity. A desire among shareholders to diversify their investment or reinvest their wealth elsewhere also may have an influence.

The Downward Liquidity Spiral. All of these danger factors can touch off a self-perpetuating "downward liquidity spiral" that will accelerate if left unchecked. (Please see Exhibit 3.) As discussed throughout this book, shareholder liquidity programs, shareholder education and other measures can prevent shareholder demands from mushrooming out of control. But in the absence of preventive measures, shareholders are likely to demand a higher current return. They discount the capital needs of the business because they see no benefit for themselves. In a family business with limited capital, this can result in a deadly liquidity spiral that drains capital from the business, which in turn causes the business to generate less cash flow and renders shareholder assets even more illiquid. Left unchecked, this downward liquidity spiral will

EXHIBIT 3 ▆▆▆▆▆▆▆▆▆▆▆▆▆▆▆▆▆▆▆▆▆▆▆▆▆▆▆▆▆▆

The Downward Liquidity Spiral

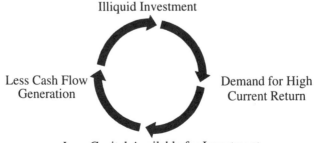

Illiquid Investment

Less Cash Flow Generation

Demand for High Current Return

Less Capital Available for Investment

™de Visscher & Company

jeopardize family control, as shown by the Family Business Triangle.

An illustration of the downward liquidity spiral at its most extreme can be found in the "fire sales" common to family businesses facing huge estate-tax bills. Shareholders' need for liquidity soars and the business is sold at a painfully deep discount — reflecting skyrocketing demands for current returns in an illiquid market.

The inverse effect can be seen in shareholders' reaction when programs are put in place to price and redeem stock. "Now that I know I can sell it, I no longer feel the need," is often the response. In other words, liquidity takes the pressure off.

Tips on Planning For Liquidity Needs. Some family businesses have successfully used techniques to help them anticipate the liquidity needs of family members. (Please see Table 3.) All are aimed at keeping management informed about shareholders' potential requirements and armed with the information and planning necessary to respond efficiently to liquidity demands.

Table 3:

TIPS ON PLANNING FOR LIQUIDITY NEEDS

1. Hold regular family meetings.

2. Hold occasional information meetings to explain significant business events and gauge holder response.

3. Stay informed on family members' personal financial, lifestyle and health status.

4. Maintain a family chart or tree to alert you to various shareholders' life stages.

5. To ease communication in larger families, organize members into intergenerational groups or branches with recognized heads of each.

6. Keep a comparative history of the business' return on equity.

7. Have a periodic valuation of the business to stay abreast of potential estate tax liability.

8. Incorporate potential liquidity needs into strategic planning for the business.

9. Maintain a list of advisory contacts and options for responding to unforeseen or emergency liquidity needs.

IV. *Managing Your Cost of Capital*

As we have seen in Section III, family businesses face innate financial pressures — limited cash, conflicting demands for shareholder liquidity and business capital, and changing needs of shareholders over the generations.

How can the business owner manage these pressures while sustaining the family business' core competitive advantage — low-cost, patient capital? **The key is to balance the cash needs of shareholders and the business at a competitive cos**t. That means analyzing and taking steps to manage your cost of capital.

Our experience shows that addressing the eventual financial expectations of shareholders sooner rather than later makes resolution more possible and less costly. The sooner the issues are addressed, the more all family members will remember that their ownership is as much an inherited privilege as it is a set of rights.

As in any business venture, an understanding of cost of capital is critical in enabling shareholders in family businesses to make sound financial decisions. Many family business owners assume that their cost of capital is the rate at which they can borrow money. But it is more than that. The other component is the investment return required to meet family shareholders' expectations.

In the following pages, we present a new formula for gauging the impact of family shareholder expectations on the capital costs of the business. (Please see Exhibit 4.) The Family Shareholder Return Formula shows how three main factors affect family shareholders' expectations. The first is the perceived risk of the family business investment. The second is liquidity. The third is the Family Effect, or the degree to which family shareholders perceive the value of family heritage and control.

The Formula's Three Fundamental Concepts. Underlying the Family Shareholder Return Formula are the three pivotal financial concepts or factors mentioned above — shareholder perceptions of risk; the important role of liquidity and the Family Effect. Before we define and apply the terms of the formula, let's take a closer look at these factors.

1. From Science to Art: Shareholder Perceptions of Risk

In business, as in life, high risk is expected to yield high rewards. If shareholders feel they are shouldering a lot of risk, they will expect high

EXHIBIT 4 ████████████████████████████████████

The Family Shareholder Return Formula

Shareholders' expected annual rate of return =
$$[RF + b(MR - RF)] * (1 + IP) * (1 - FE)$$

Definitions

RF = Risk-free rate of return, typically U.S. Treasury securities.

b = Beta expresses the volatility of the company's industry relative to the market as a whole and can be found in an investment guide. This number identifies the risk of the investment being priced poorly in relation to the market when you wish to sell.

MR = Market return, or the return expected by investors in the stock market as a whole. Historically, this long-term yield has been about 12% to 15%.

IP = Illiquidity premium, or the additional return expected by investors in instruments that can't be readily converted to cash. A highly liquid investment would have an IP of zero, leading to a neutral impact on shareholders' expected rate of return. An illiquid investment would have an IP between 0 and 1.0, increasing shareholders' expected annual rate of return as determined by the formula. Professional financial or valuation advisors can assist in determining your company's IP.

FE = Family Effect, or family members' level of satisfaction, confidence, dedication and commitment to the business. A family so satisfied that it expected no short-term returns would have an FE of one, potentially reducing shareholder expectations for current returns to zero. (Obviously, this is an extreme example.) A contentious, restless or litigious group of holders might have an FE of zero, completely wiping out the family business' core competitive advantage: a relatively low cost of capital.

---

current returns. In contrast, if they are confident in the future prospects of the business, understand the strategy and believe that management has a high likelihood of executing it well, they are more likely to be content with lower current returns.

What factors influence shareholders' perceptions of risk? Some external factors can be gauged, such as the company's vulnerability to trends in the economy and the volatility of the company's industry as a whole. But others are much more subjective: How personally confident are holders in the company, its management and its strategy? Do they believe the company has a high likelihood of executing the strategy? Do they see it as a leader in the marketplace? Do they trust the company to spot new opportunities and capitalize on them? What is their "gut feel" about the company? Do they feel like riding the waves with it? Or deserting the ship? The answers to all these questions can have a major impact on shareholder expectations, and in turn on the business' cost of equity capital.

2. The Importance of Liquidity

As in any other business investment, the ability of family business investors to sell their investment and the ease with which they can do so has a major impact on their return expectations. The less liquid the investment, the higher return the investor will require. For example, owners of a highly liquid, publicly-traded stock or bond expect a lower return than holders of less liquid investments such as real estate or units in private limited partnerships. Similarly, privately-held stocks in estate valuations are discounted for lack of marketability. This highlights once again the importance of planning liquidity programs for shareholders in family businesses.

3. The Importance of the Family Effect

In the family business, the cohesiveness and commitment of shareholders as a group — the Family Effect — is another powerful factor affecting their expectations. If shareholders are fighting, all may begin to worry about the future of the business. Dissenters sow seeds of distrust. Even if one shareholder has a controlling interest, minority holders can create enough turmoil to distract management. They may use tactics, either emotional or legal, to "bring down" those in control. If the controlling holder runs the business, he or she may be constantly worrying about what to do to get minority holders to "buy in" to strategy. Or minority holders may use or threaten litigation to make sure their concerns prevail.

In contrast, if shareholders feel like part of a united, committed team, they are likely to feel less at risk individually. Such factors as family harmony, family trust in each other, family attachment, family pride, family sense of mission and even family members' enjoyment of each other all may play a role.

If many of these conditions are strongly present, members of the shareholder team may provide support and a sense of security to each other. They are less likely to demand high current returns. As a group, such a team helps hold capital costs down, and the business' ability to create shareholder value goes up.

This is a critical concept in strategic thinking in the family business: The strength and harmony of the commitment of the ownership team. When compared with the thousands of scattered shareholders that provide the equity base of most public companies, **the potential business impact of a committed shareholder team of family members with common values and goals is potent indeed.** Good family relations in this context is like money in the bank. We call this important phenomenon "The Family Effect." (Exhibit 5.)

EXHIBIT 5 ▐▬▬▬▬▬▬▬▬▬▬▬▬▬▬▬▬▬▬▬▬▬

THE FAMILY EFFECT:
THE CORE COMPETITIVE ADVANTAGE OF FAMILY BUSINESS

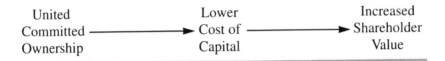

| United Committed Ownership | → | Lower Cost of Capital | → | Increased Shareholder Value |

The Family Effect in Action. While the Family Effect can be a family business' biggest advantage, a breakdown of the Family Effect can quickly become its biggest disadvantage. Consider these two fictional scenarios from separate family businesses with roughly similar financial performance and strategic outlooks:

Company A

Carl, 32, a grand-nephew of the founder of Print-It Corp., holds a five percent stake in the business, which is in its third generation of family ownership and management. Carl remembers how important the business was to his father, who worked full-time as its controller until he retired at age 72. But Carl, a software engineer for a different company, feels little connection to the business, which is now managed by two cousins and a team of nonfamily managers. He knows few of its employees and nothing of its long-term strategy. The dividends on the stock he inherited at his father's death haven't changed for as long as he can remember. Worse yet, his cousins in the business are squabbling and family gatherings are increasingly marred by complaints about low dividends. Carl has heard from a friend in town that two family managers are trying to plan a buyout. At Thanksgiving, another cousin quietly began soliciting support from dissident shareholders for replacing management. More and more frequently, Carl wishes he could sell his stock, but he knows of no market for it.

Company B

Carol, 41, inherited a stake in Jones Inc., the family printing business, from her father, who was one of a team of four third-generation managers. In her work as a lawyer, Carol is far removed from the business. But as one of 35 shareholders, she attends quarterly family meetings, where she has learned that the business' long-term strategy is to acquire a leading market share in an increasing number of regional markets, primarily through acquisition. She helped research a family history project on how family values, such as fairness to customers and philanthropic activity in the community, had been transmitted through the generations and manifested in the business. And she made suggestions to a family committee that is drafting a family mission statement, expressing the family's long-term goals for both the family and the business. Though acquisitions sometimes drain capital and are one reason dividends remain low, Carol understands managers' investment goals and is confident, based on results in the company's current markets, that the business stands a good chance of achieving them. And she feels proud when professional contacts ask her if she is associated with the business, which still carries the family name.

Each of the above companies has similar business prospects. But Carl and Carol perceive those prospects completely differently. Carl feels he is on a slippery slope, at risk of losing much or most of his equity investment. Without a ready market for his stock, he is likely to take what he sees as the next best route to keeping himself whole financially — demanding either redemption of his shares or higher dividends, regardless of the impact on the business. The cost to the business of meeting such demands from Carl and others like him seems certain to skyrocket out of control.

Carol, on the other hand, feels confident about the future of the business. She trusts other family members and believes she shares their vision. She also enjoys and takes pride in her association with them. She thinks of the business as a long-term investment, and looks forward to participating in its future growth.

In these two cases, shareholder perceptions are having major impacts on costs of capital. By providing patient capital, Carol embodies the Family Effect, exponentially increasing the economic power of her family business, and her family, in the process. Carl, on the other hand, reflects a collective shareholder uneasiness and suspicion that seems certain to create a downward liquidity spiral. Left unchecked, it could render the business uncompetitive and destroy family control.

The Family Effect influences the business' cost of capital in other ways as well. One way to lower cost of capital is to raise the proportion of debt used for financing — more leverage. But both borrowers and lenders must be willing to do that before it can happen. This is where the Family Effect again comes into play. A lender is more likely to be willing to lend money at relatively low rates to a business with a cohesive, confident, committed base of family shareholders who view the business as a long-term investment. The lower the apparent risk, the more lenders will be willing to lend. Similarly, **shareholders who are confident in management and planning on long-term gains are more likely to be willing to take on more debt.** Under the right circumstances, this can reduce a business' cost of capital — increasing its ability to compete and to create shareholder value.

Bringing It All Together: The Interaction of Risk, Liquidity and the Family Effect. As mentioned earlier, the interaction of shareholders' perceptions of risk, shareholder liquidity and the Family Effect is illustrated in the Family Shareholder Return Formula. Let's revisit the formula to define its components more specifically and see how it can be applied as a planning and analytical tool. As shown in Exhibit 4, the first part of the equation incorporates factors that affect any stock on publicly traded markets. The second part reflects factors specific to family businesses.

Here is how the formula would apply in two contrasting situations:

Case A: A public company in the consumer food business. The rate on 10-year Treasury instruments is, say, 8 percent before taxes. The stock market, as measured by the average total return on equity of the Standard & Poor's 500-stock index, is yielding 15 percent before taxes. (That includes both dividends and stock-price appreciation.) The beta typically applied to food stocks is 1 because food stocks are as stable as the overall economy. The stock, because it is traded on the New York Stock Exchange and is highly liquid, commands no illiquidity premium. And the Family Effect, of course, is zero in the case of its thousands of unrelated, widely dispersed shareholders. Here's how the formula would look:

$$\text{Shareholder Required Rate of Return} =$$
$$[8\% + 1(15\% - 8\%)] * (1 + 0) * (1 - 0) = 15\%$$

Predictably, the formula shows that shareholders in this company expect current returns to at least match the performance of the stock market as a whole.

24

Case B: A family business in the same industry. This third-generation enterprise, like most family businesses, has no programs in place to provide liquidity to shareholders, establishing an illiquidity premium for purposes of the equation of 0.35. The company also has made no attempt to inform, educate or unify shareholders. One branch of the family, made up of only inactive shareholders, has begun to pressure managers in the business for a dividend increase and has raised questions among members about whether managers' compensation is unfairly high. While the tensions aren't likely to explode into litigation any time soon, the uneasiness is rising, indicating a Family Effect of 0.10 for the purposes of the equation.

Here's how the formula would apply to this company:

Shareholder Required Rate of Return =
[8% + 1(15% - 8%)] * (1 + 0.35) * (1 - 0.10) =
[15%] * (1.35) * (0.90) = 18.23%.

Shareholders in this business might be expected, then, to demand a return not only equal to, but *greater than,* shareholders might expect in public stock markets. This business' failure to provide for holders' liquidity needs coupled with its shaky family ties and commitment have seriously weakened its core competitive advantage: patient capital. This could cripple the business as it tries to compete against increasingly muscular, well-financed global competitors.

Case C: A different family business in the same industry.

Let's take a look at a third company, a family business in the same industry that has taken steps to provide shareholder liquidity and build strong family relations and commitment. This company provides both an annual opportunity for family members to redeem a limited amount of shares, as discussed later in this book, and a company-guaranteed shareholder loan program, suggesting an illiquidity premium of only about 0.2. It also has managed to build a strong shareholder base like the one described previously in the example of Carol's company, Jones Inc., suggesting a Family Effect of 0.6.

Here is what the formula tells us about the company's required shareholder rate of return:

Shareholder Required Rate of Return =
[8% + 1(15% - 8%)] * (1 + 0.2) * (1 - 0.6) =
[15%] * (1.2) * (0.4) = 7.2%.

Not only has this company nearly wiped out the illiquidity premium that can increase a family business' capital costs, it also has capitalized on a core advantage of family businesses — the Family Effect — to slash its cost of capital well below that of its big, publicly-held competitors.

Again, effective shareholder communication and good family relations are like money in the bank.

The Relationship Between the Illiquidity Premium and the Family Effect. As suggested earlier, there is a relationship between the Illiquidity Premium and the Family Effect. To some extent, measures taken to increase liquidity, such as annual redemption programs, loan programs and other efforts, can increase the Family Effect. In other words, providing liquidity to shareholders can offset a certain degree of family dissatisfaction.

Conversely, increasing the Family Effect can make up for a degree of shareholder illiquidity. If family members are cohesive, content with their investment and willing to wait for long-term strategies to yield long-term gains, they are less likely to feel dissatisfied at the illiquidity of their holdings.

Maximizing the Family Effect. Often, fostering **the Family Effect requires conscious, planned effort as a business passes through successive generations of family ownership.**

Clearly, it is in the best interest of the business and the family to make this effort. Though in-depth treatment of this subject is beyond the scope of this book, it may be helpful to **keep four principles in mind: good family communication; shareholder education; cultivating a sense of shared interests; and fostering an awareness of shared values.** Other volumes in the **Family Business Leadership Series**, including *Family Meetings: How to Build a Stronger Family and a Stronger Business*, and *How Families Work Together*, address some of these issues. Meanwhile, specific steps that can be used to maximize the Family Effect are shown in Table 4.

Good Communication. Good communication among family members is imperative and often is fostered by family meetings. Shareholder education at these meetings and through periodic seminars and retreats can help shareholders develop a sense of shared interests. Some business owners review with holders such questions as: How do we see the value of our business increasing? What issues do we see on the horizon? What are future risks to the value of our business? What decisions are we going to have to make in the future? How are our industry and the world changing in ways that will affect us?

Shared Interest and Values. A sense of shared interests and values also has tremendous potential for increasing the Family Effect. Educating shareholders about the business can help them understand

Table 4: _____

> ### TIPS ON MAXIMIZING THE FAMILY EFFECT
>
> - Hold regular family meetings
> - Develop shareholder education programs
> - Review business results with family members
> - Talk with family about business trends and strategy
> - Review trends in shareholder value with family
> - Discuss the responsibility of the business to its constituencies, including shareholders, customers, employees, suppliers and the community at large
> - Prepare a family mission statement
> - Set up a family bank (described in Section VI)
> - Hold social gatherings as a family
> - Research and write a family history
> - Hold family celebrations such as a Founder's Day picnic
> - Organize a family foundation or family office
> - Develop and honor meaningful family traditions or rituals
> - Develop a statement of family values and discuss how to manifest those values in the business

that their stake in its long-term performance is held in common. Discussing how the business treats employees, suppliers, customers and the community at large can encourage family members to think this way. Family pride in the business' responsible, stewardlike treatment of all constituencies can be a powerful unifying factor.

Mission statements also can build a sense of family purpose that transcends short-term results. For example, some families name in these statements such goals as nurturing entrepreneurship among family members, serving the community through philanthropy, or setting an example of ethical business conduct.

Family gatherings that blend having fun together with learning about the business can nurture all these bonds — communication, education, and a sense of shared interests and values — fortifying the Family Effect across the generations.

Shareholder Education. These sessions also afford an opportunity to help shareholders understand some important principles of running a successful business. These issues may arise in discussing such questions as, "Where does all the cash go?" and, "Why do we always act as if money is tight?" Table 5 contains a framework for shareholder education, in the form of four important financial questions shareholders should be educated and encouraged to ask.

Table 5:

Four Important Financial Questions
Shareholders Should be Encouraged to Ask

1. What is our total return on investment — the best index of how well we're creating value?

2. How much money is the business spending to create growth and future profits?

3. What percentage of our profit is needed to fund new growth — for working capital and for new fixed assets?

4. What percentage of the profit that we keep in the business will Uncle Sam eventually take in death taxes?

V. *To Sell or Not to Sell*

As discussed earlier, a primary goal for family businesses should be to maintain control over decisionmaking. One question that often comes up as family business owners weigh various options is whether to sell the business.

In some cases, selling is probably the right choice. The family may lack capable successors and be unwilling or unable to look for non-family leadership. Sale of the business may promise an irresistibly high price. Selling out and reinvesting the proceeds may offer a better chance to multiply wealth (though it rarely does). Or shareholders may decide they want to diversify their assets beyond what ownership of a family business will allow (though again, they may underestimate the risk of other alternatives). But there are at least as many logical — though less obvious — reasons not to sell. (Please see Table 6.)

As many families have experienced, family business ownership can be an outstanding opportunity to generate wealth for family members across generations. Keeping a healthy business and reinvesting the earnings over the years can yield sharply higher net proceeds in the future than selling the business. Consider the actual case of an electrical-controls manufacturer — let's call it "The Voltage Co." This Subchapter S corporation is nearly debt-free. But Voltage is not a fast-growing business. Sales, at $25 million annually, are growing at about three percent a year in real terms, barely keeping pace with inflation. Annual dividends have totalled about 40 percent of pretax earnings, which were $1.5 million in the latest year. The business is valued at about $8.0 million or five times pretax profit.

Depending on market conditions, the owners of this business might logically consider selling it. The sale of the business would net $4.8 million, after taxes, to the shareholders, and the future value of those after-tax proceeds after 20 years, assuming a reinvestment rate of 7 percent, would be $18.5 million (Please see Table 7.)

Why Not Sell? One reason not to sell is that a bare-bones financial projection — even assuming that the business does no better than its current modest growth rate — shows that its owners could be collectively wealthier by nearly 50 percent if they waited 20 more years to sell the business. As shown in Table 7, total shareholder wealth generated from

Table 6: ───────────────────────────────

WEIGHING SALE OF THE FAMILY BUSINESS

Why Some Families Choose to Sell Their Businesses	Why Some Families Choose to Retain Their Businesses
■ Lack of capable successors	■ Potential of family business as a wealth creation vehicle
■ Lack of capital to grow business	■ Family pride in ownership
■ Threat from large, well-financed competitors	■ Competitive advantage of staying private
■ Shareholder liquidity demands	■ Business ownership as valuable component of family heritage
■ Estate tax burden	■ Desire to pass on opportunities to children
■ Lure of high prices on private or public markets	■ Role of business in keeping family together
■ Promise of greater wealth by reinvesting assets	■ Fear that passive wealth can harm family values and work ethic
■ Shareholder desire to diversify investment for higher return	■ Concern that investing in new areas is more risky than maintaining business

---

a sale of the business 20 years in the future would be $27.7 million — nearly half again as much as the $18.5 million earned through the earlier sale of the business. And this projection excludes one very important financial reward of business ownership: 20 additional years of salaries, benefits and perks for family members working in the business.

Management Advantages of Staying Private. There also are sound management reasons for sustaining private ownership. Private status avoids the reporting requirements imposed on companies that sell stock to the public. When the family owners of one well-known specialty food concern needed to meet the liquidity needs of one branch of the family,

Table 7: _____

THE WEALTH-GENERATING POTENTIAL OF SELLING NOW VS. RETAINING THE BUSINESS LONGER THE VOLTAGE CO.[1]	
Option 1: Sell Business Now[2]	**Option 2: Sell Business in 20 Years [2]**
Net Sale Proceeds **$4.8 MM**[3]	Annual Sales in 20 Years **$45.2 MM**[4]
	Future Annual Earnings **2.7 MM**[5]
	Fair Market Value **14.4 MM**[3]
	Net Sale Proceeds **8.6 MM**
Future Value of Proceeds after 20 Years **$18.5 MM**	Value of 20 Years' Dividends Reinvested **19.1 MM**
	Total Wealth Created After 20 Years **$27.7 MM**

(1) Not its real name.

(2) Assuming 40% tax rate and 7% net reinvestment rate of return.

(3) Assuming sale price of five times earnings before interest and taxes.

(4) Assuming continued 3% annual sales growth.

(5) Before interest and taxes.

they consulted advisors who offered them two choices: sell out or go public. The family didn't want to sell out, so the company sold stock to the public.

Today, family executives of the business say that if they had known then what they know now, they never would have gone public. First, they didn't really need to tap public markets; the company hasn't raised any capital on public markets since the initial public offering. Even more important, they have found it harder to compete as a public company. Reporting requirements are burdensome, and the need to divulge such sensitive issues as operating margins and acquisition plans make the requirements even harder to manage.

Benefits for the Family of Retaining Ownership. Business ownership brings intangible advantages, too, of course, some of which were discussed in No. 2 of the **Family Business Leadership Series**, *Family Meetings: How to Build a Stronger Family and a Stronger Business*. Many business owners see major advantages to their families in passing on ownership of a business from generation to generation. **Business ownership can be a major source of family pride and an important component of a family's sense of heritage.** It can afford irreplaceable career and personal growth opportunities to future generations. As a focal point for generating shared goals and interests, the family business can play an important role in keeping the family together. And it can provide a unique vehicle for manifesting family values and goals in the community.

VI. Financial Solutions:
Maintaining Family Control Through The Generations

We have discussed in previous sections of this book some important principles of managing your liquidity needs and cost of capital.

The final section outlines a variety of financial tools designed to help you meet liquidity and capital needs in a planned fashion. While some of the techniques are most useful to larger businesses, many can be applied in various forms to smaller businesses as well. All are designed to help the business owner, in keeping with the vision articulated at the beginning of this book by entrepreneur Sam Johnson, make the most of the financial resources at hand while maximizing the opportunity for future generations to do the same.

Principles at Work in Planning Transitions. The business owner should keep five principles in mind when weighing financial solutions. The best techniques are fair to all shareholders, including those who remain in the business. One family business, for instance, was planning to buy out several inactive shareholders by borrowing a large amount of money, leaving the company highly leveraged. While this plan provided shareholders participating in the buyout with what they deemed a "fair price," it was unfair to those who remained in the business. They were left with a company saddled with a large amount of debt.

Second, financial solutions must provide adequate capital to sustain a healthy business. As described in Section III of this booklet, a failure to meet shareholders' liquidity needs in a sustainable, long-term way encourages holders to focus on current returns. This in turn leaves less capital available for investment, weakening the business and generating less cash flow that in turn leaves less cash available for shareholders' liquidity needs. Sound financial solutions must reverse this downward liquidity spiral.

Third, some financial solutions may be based on plans to shift from 100 percent family ownership of the business to family control of the business. This step may be necessary to sustain business growth without allowing the family business triangle discussed earlier to collapse, destroying family control.

Fourth, financial solutions must be adaptable to the unique needs of each business.

Fifth, successful financial solutions always include programs to inform and education shareholders about the solution and the reason for it. These communications can do much to enhance the Family Effect, as discussed above. An annual stock repurchase program, for instance, can provide an occasion for an annual presentation to the family on the value of the business, its strategy and its mission in relation to shareholders, employees and others.

Sixth, all solutions involving the redemption of shares must be carefully planned with respect to tax implications of transactions. A single transaction can impact individual income, estate and capital gains taxes and corporate income taxes. Clearly, planning for liquidity and capital needs requires expert advice from financial and legal professionals.

Financial Solutions: Meeting Liquidity and Capital Needs

The following section describes twenty-two techniques for meeting capital and liquidity needs. The first group of eleven requires no outside capital, while the second group does involve outside capital sources. All are summarized in Table 8 and described in greater detail in the text that follows.

TABLE 8
SOLUTIONS FOR LIQUIDITY AND CAPITAL NEEDS

PART I: INTERNAL SOLUTIONS REQUIRING NO OUTSIDE CAPITAL

1. PAYMENTS OF DIVIDENDS

Definition: *Distributing a Portion of earnings to holders*

Advantages: ■ Helps meet shareholder liquidity needs

Disadvantages: ■ Drains business capital
■ No educational components for shareholders
■ Can foster sense of entitlement

2. COMPANY CLEARINGHOUSE

Definition: *Company acts as an information clearinghouse for holders who want to buy or sell shares. No price-setting or guarantees are provided*

Advantages: ■ Simple low-cost method
■ Helpful to shareholders who don't know each other

Disadvantages: ■ Offers little advantage to small shareholder groups
■ No agreed-upon stock pricing formula, so that prices set in private transactions may have major estate and gift tax ramifications for other holders
■ No assurance to sellers that buyer will be found

Definition: *Company arranges for commercial banks to lend shareholders money using their stock in the business as collateral*

Advantages:
- Enables shareholders to gain liquidity without selling their stock
- Appeals to lenders because loans are guaranteed, either formally or informally, by the company
- Affords younger holders an opportunity to learn financial responsibility

Disadvantages:
- Reduces capacity of the business to borrow money by obligating it to back loans to shareholders
- Requires company to assume risk that holder may default, forcing it to repay loan to avoid forfeiture of shares to lender
- Risks unequal treatment of shareholders by exposing all to the risk that some may default

Definition: *A program enabling shareholders to sell stock to other holders or the company within a set time period each year at a price established by formula*

Advantages:
- Provides immediate and ongoing liquidity to shareholders
- Establishes a fair and equitable valuation formula for stock
- Through annual approval process, balances liquidity needs of holders with capital needs of business.

Disadvantages:
- Requires setting aside part of cash flow for an annual redemption plan
- Tax-treatment for redeeming and non-redeeming shareholders can be disadvantageous unless properly structured

Definition: *The business repurchases shares in installments rather than with a lumpsum payment*

Advantages:
- Locks in sale price for stock at beginning of payment period
- Useful in repurchasing shares in estate settlements and other emergency situations

Disadvantages:
- Too complex to manage repurchases from more than one or two shareholders
- IRS rules place limits on installment repurchases, especially in settling an estate

Definition: *The company redeems stock in exchange for a company asset*

Advantages: ■ Allows redemptions without draining cash from the company
■ Allows company to match individual interests of shareholders with property used in redemption
■ Allows company to lock in value of appreciating asset

Disadvantages: ■ Negative tax implications
■ Potential for disputes if the company still depends upon or uses the assets exchanged

Definition: *Company sets up a trust to buy stock from shareholders for benefit of employees*

Advantages: ■ Tax advantages to shareholders
■ Involves employees as shareholders

Disadvantages: ■ Creates repurchase liability for the company if employees retire or leave the company
■ Involves employees as shareholders
■ Typically establishes low valuation of stock

Definition: *Dividing assets among shareholders, usually through an exchange of shares in sister companies*

Advantages: ■ Allows company to match cash flow and appreciation of assets with individual preferences and needs of shareholders
■ Tax free

Disadvantages: ■ Difficult to accomplish if businesses or assets are interdependent
■ Potential for shareholder conflict over performance of assets
■ Requires comprehensive information to shareholders
■ May have estate tax consequences if separation of assets results in higher valuation

Definition: *Tax-advantaged exchange of stock among shareholders to match holder groups' objective for current income vs. future return*

Advantages: ■ Can enable separation of future appreciation in stock value from current income for estate tax purposes

■ Allows separation of voting and non-voting shares between active and inactive holders

■ Can serve as incentive for active shareholders by capturing future appreciation of stock in voting shares, while non-voting shares are paid more current income

Disadvantages: ■ Potentially negative tax implications

■ Requires independent valuation of each new class of stock created

■ Doesn't provide holders immediate liquidity but merely creates a basis for increased current income in the future

Definition: *Payment of previously taxed retained earnings in an S corporation to holders*

Advantages: ■ Avoids double taxation of profit that applies to C corporations

Disadvantages: ■ Does not allow for unequal distribution to reflect shareholders' differing individual tax liabilities

Definition: *Setting up a fund to finance entrepreneurial ventures of shareholders*

Advantages: ■ Diversifies assets of the company

■ Provides potential to generate new family capital through entrepreneurial ventures

■ Educates family members in creating, executing and financing entrepreneurial ideas

■ Promotes family working together

Disadvantages: ■ Ties up business capital for other uses

■ Risks creating shareholder resentment over perceived inequalities of treatment

■ Creates potential for conflict over which shareholder proposals are funded

■ Creates potential for conflict over repayment terms

■ Requires family to share risk of individuals' ventures

A. BORROWING MONEY

Definition: *Borrowing money secured by assets or personal guarantee*

Sources: ■ Commercial lender

Advantages: ■ Flexibility to be structured either as a term loan or revolving credit

Disadvantages: ■ Repayment terms must match duration of the business' need for capital

Definition: *Privately arranged lending agreements involving senior, subordinate or term debt, usually for 10- to 15-year maturities*

Sources: ■ Banks, insurance companies, pension funds or other institutional investors, sometimes identifiable through local economic development authorities

Advantages: ■ Flexibility
■ Private transactions avoid regulatory requirements for public sale of debt

Disadvantages: ■ Usually includes restrictive covenants
■ May not be available for smaller businesses
■ May require securitization of assets or personal guarantees

Definition: *Same as ESOP described above, except the company borrows money to finance purchases of stock from holders*

Sources: ■ Banks or other lenders

Advantages: ■ Same as ESOP

Disadvantages: ■ Same as ESOP
■ Reduces borrowing capacity of the company

Definition: *Same as recapitalization described above, except the company borrows money to finance exchange of shares*

Sources: ■ Banks, insurance companies, or other institutional investors

Advantages: ■ Same as recapitalization described above

Disadvantages: ■ Same as recapitalization described above
■ Reduces borrowing capacity of the company

B. SALE OF ASSETS

Definition: *Self-evident*

Sources: ■ Any qualified buyer

Advantages: ■ May trim non-strategic assets or other property not essential to operations
■ Raises cash without changing ownership structure or losing family control
■ Raises cash without raising debt-equity ratio

Disadvantages: ■ Requires new business arrangements with owners of assets still in use by company

Definition: *Incorporating a division or operation of the company and selling it outright*

Sources: ■ Any qualified buyer

Advantages: ■ Raises cash without changing ownership structure or losing family control
■ Raises cash without raising debt-equity ratio
■ Under some conditions, may trim nonstrategic assets or other property not essential to operations

Disadvantages: ■ Separating a subsidiary from the holding company may be complex or difficult
■ May have negative tax consequences

C. FINDING AN EQUITY PARTNER

Definition: *Equity investment by an individual or other entity*

Sources: ■ Acquaintances, relatives, pension funds, insurance companies, equity investment funds, mezzanine funds, banks

Advantages: ■ Allows family control
■ Flexible in structure
■ Less expensive to structure than IPO
■ Minority partner may provide an ongoing market for family stock

Disadvantages: ■ Investor may require rights to take control if certain targets are not met
■ Investor may require option to be bought by a certain time
■ Anti-dilution provisions may restrict issuance of new stock
■ Typically requires higher ongoing rate of total return to investor than the public market

Definition: *Incorporating a division or operation of the company and offering stock in it to the public*

Sources: ■ Public markets via investment bankers

Advantages: ■ Allows company to tap public markets without taking the whole company public
■ Creates a new "acquisition currency" for the family business, which can be used to make acquisitions or buy other assets

Disadvantages: ■ Separating a subsidiary from the holding company may be complex or difficult
■ May have negative tax consequences
■ Available subsidiaries may not be large enough for IPO
■ Regulatory requirements associated with IPO can be costly or burdensome

Definition: *A cooperative arrangement between two or more companies which pool resources to pursue a common strategy*

Sources: ■ Other family businesses or other companies in North America or overseas. Financial groups with compatible assets

Advantages: ■ Sharing of risk with future generations
■ Leverages differing resources and capabilities of partners
■ Extends partners' geographic reach
■ Provides relatively low-cost capital because of mutual advantages to partners
■ Can ease access to outside management

Disadvantages: ■ Requires realistic feasibility study and risk analysis
■ Requires extensive due diligence
■ Requires clear definition of partners' roles
■ Breakdown in trust or communication can jeopardize arrangement

■■■

Definition: *Equity investment in selected assets of the business by an individual or financial entity*

Sources: ■ Acquaintances, relatives, pension funds, insurance companies, equity investment funds, venture capital funds, banks

Advantages: ■ Flexible financing tool
■ Partner may provide an ongoing source of liquidity for shareholders
■ Allows family control

Disadvantages: ■ May be difficult to attract a joint venture partner
■ Investor may require right to take control if targets are not met

■■■

Definition: *Using outside capital to set up new branches or outlets of the business that will be operated by the family business*

Sources: ■ Individuals or other outside investors

Advantages: ■ Leverages family business capabilities using outside capital
■ Allows family control

Disadvantages: ■ May be difficult to attract syndication partners
■ Relationships must be structured carefully, defining roles, shared risks

I. Internal Solutions

Many family businesses prefer when possible to finance shareholder liquidity needs internally. A notable exception: In some situations, a certain amount of borrowing from outside sources, or leverage, is necessary to ensure an adequate return on equity to shareholders.

The following eleven techniques are designed primarily to meet shareholder liquidity needs through internal funds. In addition to the techniques shown here, many family businesses have satisfied shareholders' requirements through salaries, perks or tapping the cash surrender value of life insurance. All of these techniques can be useful and may be combined with the solutions shown below.

When the primary need is for additional capital for the business, soluions that require external financing, such as those presented in the section after this one, are usually required.

1. Payment of Dividends

Definition: Periodic distribution of a portion of earnings to shareholders, based on such factors as the business' cash flow, shareholders' expectations regarding their rate of return, and the level of return available on competing investments.

Purpose: Meeting shareholder liquidity needs.

Pros: The most common method used for meeting liquidity needs. Relatively simple and predictable.

Cons: Drains capital from the business. Provides shareholders no educational benefits or sense of participation in the business. Risks fostering a sense of entitlement among shareholders if dividend increases continue with no shareholder education about the responsibilities conveyed by business ownership.

2. Company Clearinghouse

Definition: A mechanism whereby the company acts as a stock exchange or clearinghouse for buyers and sellers of stock to meet. No prices are set or guaranteed and the company assumes no financial risk or obligation.

Purpose: To facilitate desired sales of stock, providing needed liquidity for shareholders.

Pros: Simple, low in cost and entails no financial commitment by the company. Particularly helpful in linking shareholders who don't know each other.

Cons: Lack of guarantees that buyers will be found or shareholders' liquidity needs will be met. Also, poses potentially negative tax consequences for all shareholders by generating prices on private transactions that may distort the value of stock for gift or estate tax purposes.

3. Company-Sponsored Loan Program

Definition: An arrangement by the company for a commercial bank or other entity to lend shareholders money using their stock in the family business as collateral. The company may formally guarantee the loans, or its involvement may act as an informal guarantee.

Purpose: To provide liquidity for shareholders.

Pros: Available to any family business with borrowing capacity. Enables shareholders to gain liquidity without selling their stock. Can afford shareholders, particularly younger ones, an opportunity to learn responsibility for making regular loan repayments and managing their money.

Cons: Ties up some of the company's credit capacity. Provides no guarantee that the company's credit capacity will be adequate to equitably meet requests from all family members who may desire loans. Exposes all shareholders to any credit problems individual family members may have.

(To eliminate some of these disadvantages, the company may use retained earnings to lend shareholders money or, in smaller but successful family businesses, senior family members may provide funds for loans. If retained earnings are used, the company loses access to some of its capital.)

4. Annual Shareholder Redemption Plan

Definition: A method that enables shareholders to sell stock to other shareholders or, if no purchasers are available, to the company during a set period each year, at a price set by a formula. A portion of the company's annual cash flow is set aside to finance purchases by the company.

Purpose: To provide regular opportunities for shareholders to gain liquidity by redeeming shares.

Pros: Provides a fair and consistent basis for shareholders to see how the company is doing through the annual process of valuing the stock. Because annual board approval is required, provides a means for balancing the liquidity needs of holders with the capital needs of the business. Assures shareholders of an opportunity to raise cash regularly, often easing worries and potentially reducing shareholder expectations for current return.

Cons: Requires setting aside part of the company's cash flow to repurchase shares. Requires effort and oversight, including an annual valuation of shares. (Please see Exhibit 6.)

One word of caution regarding redemption plan relates to two IRS provisions, which can create significant tax liabilities for redeeming and non-redeeming shareholders, if the redemption plans are not structured properly.

It is not the purpose of this book to enter into legality tax discussions. Suffice to say that in all cases we would suggest to obtain highly qualified tax counseling.

Just very briefly, under current IRS provisions, redemptions by selling shares back to the corporation will be taxed as a dividend at ordinary income tax rates, unless the redemption falls within some very specific criteria. Additionally, "family attribution rules" make it difficult for a family business to fall within those IRS guidelines of capital gains treatments. So once again proper tax advice in this area is essential.

The second IRS provision affecting redemption could have a very negative effect on the non-redeeming shareholders. As such, a redemption transaction which results in increasing the ownership interest of the non-redeeming shareholders (which most redemptions to the corporation do), maybe viewed by the IRS as a constructive distribution and taxed as such to those non-redeeming shareholders. There are several ways of preventing the applicability of those two provisions. An example would be to use a liquidity agent or outside redemption maker to affect the redemption. But there again, competent tax advice is essential!

EXHIBIT 6 ██

Timing of Annual Redemption Plan
Example of Annual Time Schedule

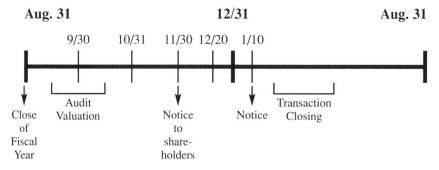

de Visscher & Company

The formula price is affirmed annually, usually by the board of directors. A cumulative redemption fund financed by the company's cash flow also is approved by the board annually. The unused portion is carried over to the following year.

A limited time period is set during which stock can be redeemed each year, concentrating buying and selling activity to ensure maximum liquidity. One way of timing a redemption program is shown in Exhibit 6. In this example, an annual audit and valuation of the business begins about two weeks after the close of the fiscal year and is completed in a little more than two months. The first notice to shareholders of the opportunity to sell shares and the formula price for the year goes out at the end of the first fiscal quarter. Shareholders have 20 days to respond. A second shareholder notice goes out a little over two weeks later with information about making transactions. Actual redemptions and matching of buyers and sellers take place within about six weeks during the fiscal second quarter.

5. Installment Repurchases of Stock

Definition: An agreement by the company to repurchase stock under an installment method rather than by a lump sum. Under this method, the company agrees with the selling shareholder or his or her estate to repurchase the stock at a fixed price in installments over a number of years, typically three to five. It can be done by using a redemption fund, as described earlier, or by simply using the company's cash flow.

Purpose: Provides a way for the company to meet relatively large demands for liquidity in planned stages.

Pros: Affords the company the opportunity to lock in a price for stock that may be appreciating. Enables the company to buy shares if it doesn't have 100 percent of the purchase price available, easing the financial drain on the company. Can be particularly useful in such cases as the death of a key shareholder whose survivors need cash to pay estate taxes.

Cons: Can be very difficult and complex if several shareholders are involved. May be affected by IRS rules on installment repurchases, particularly in estate situations.

6. Redemptions of Stock for Property

Definition: This technique enables shareholders to redeem their stock in exchange for an asset of the company instead of cash.

Purpose: Provides shareholder liquidity.

Pros: Available to any company with assets that can be separated from the business. Enables the company to lock in the value of appreciating asset outside the company. Allows use of various kinds of assets, including real estate or even intellectual property such as patents. Avoids draining cash from the company. Allows the company to match the kind of asset with the interests and desires of individual shareholders, providing, for instance, real estate in return for stock owned by a shareholder interested in real estate.

Cons: Can have negative tax implications, with the company and the shareholders both potentially incurring a capital gains tax liability, in addition to a potential sales tax liability for the company. Raises the potential for conflict of interest if the company continues to use the assets exchanged for stock.

7. Employee Stock Ownership Plan

Definition: This technique entails setting up a trust that makes annual stock purchases from shareholders for the benefit of employees, either with internal cash flow or, as discussed later, with borrowed funds.

Purpose: Once an ESOP owns 30 percent or more of the company's stock, shareholders can gain liquidity by selling stock to the ESOP on a tax-deferred basis.

Pros: Can provide tax advantages for shareholders. Involves employees as stockholders of the company, which can be either an advantage or disadvantage depending on the circumstances.

Cons: Involves employees as stockholders of the company. Not a practical technique for companies of all sizes because an ESOP entails considerable expenses, including initial costs for setting it up and ongoing costs for qualification with the IRS, stock appraisals, recordkeeping and possible government audits. Typically obligates the company to repurchase shares from employees when they retire or leave the company, assuming their interest in the ESOP is vested, potentially causing a cash drain. Provides relatively low valuations of stock, diminishing some of the benefits for family shareholders.

8. Split-Up of Assets

Definition: Dividing assets of the business among shareholders, usually by exchanging stock for shares in sister companies or in subsidiaries of a holding company.

Purpose: To tailor family members' holdings to their individual liquidity needs and investment goals.

Pros: Can be accomplished tax-free. Allows the company to match the cash flow and appreciation potential of various assets with individual shareholders' differing preferences and needs.

Cons: Can be difficult to structure. Can hurt family relations if some shareholders are better informed than others and wind up owning the better-performing assets, making essential both careful efforts to inform all shareholders as well as independent valuations of the assets

lender in the form of either a revolving credit or a term loan. The debt is typically secured either by assets or a personal guarantee.

Purpose: To provide business capital.

Pros: A flexible and accessible financing tool.

Cons: To hold down borrowing costs, requires matching the term of the loan to the nature of the investment being made. (Many family businesses make the mistake of financing long-term investments with short-term credit lines, causing potential cash flow problems when the money must be repaid before the investment begins to show a return.)

A2. Private Placement of Debt

Definition: This typically involves borrowing money privately from financial institutions in the form of senior or subordinated debt or a revolving credit line. Lenders might include banks, insurance companies, pension funds, other institutional investors or even individuals willing to become involved in this way with smaller businesses. Maturities of term loans usually range from ten to fifteen years, and interest rates typically float in relation to an index such as the prime rate.

Purpose: Capital to be used for a wide range of purposes.

Pros: Offers many options in structuring debt to meet the needs of the business.

Cons: Typically places restrictive covenants on the borrower that can be quite rigid, including terms and repayment schedules. May require securitization of assets or personal guarantees.

A3. Leveraged ESOP

Definition: This method has all the same characteristics as the ESOP described earlier, except it involves borrowing money from a bank or other lender to finance purchase of stock from shareholders.

A4. Leveraged recapitalization

Definition: This technique has all the same characteristics as the recapitalization described earlier, except it entails borrowing money to execute the restructuring.

B. Sale of Assets

B1. Sale of Real Estate or Other Assets

Definition: This technique entails divesting assets to raise business capital. Amid signs of a fundamental shift toward flat or falling prices for commercial real state in many regions of North America, many companies are selling real estate in particular.

Pros: Fits well with a strategy trimming nonstrategic assets. Has the advantage of raising cash without changing the business' ownership structure or debt ratios. Can eliminate distractions for management, helping focus attention on core operating businesses.

Cons: Often requires making new leasing or other arrangements with new owners of the assets, potentially raising new hurdles.

B2. Sale of Subsidiary
Definition: This technique involves sale of a business unit.
Purpose: Raising cash for business capital or to meet liquidity needs.
Pros: Permits continuation of family control of the main business.
Cons: May be difficult to separate a division or operation for sale. May create unforeseen tax liabilities or have negative implications for future business relationships.

C. Finding an Equity Partner
C1. Private Equity
Definition: This method involves transferring stock to an individual or other investor, ranging from a relative or friend to another family business, a pension fund, insurance company, venture capital fund or other financial entity. Private equity agreements typically convey to the investor preferred stock that is convertible to common at a one-for-one ratio and provide dividends, representation on the company's board and rights to financial information, among other things.

Private equity can come from various sources depending on the size of the family business. Individual investors or regional venture capitalists may be an appropriate source for smaller firms. On the other hand, larger companies would typically turn to financial institutions such as insurance companies or pension funds.

Purpose: Provides capital for a wide range of business purposes, including shareholder liquidity.

Pros: Allows access to a private equity market that has grown to an estimated $3 billion to $5 billion in North American and overseas. Affords liquidity while sustaining family control. Allows flexibility, providing primary capital, for use to create immediate liquidity; or provides secondary capital, to replace capital provided by existing shareholders, or both. Costs less and is less onerous to structure than a public offering. Engenders a minority partner relationship that may provide a variety of resources, from support for the business' long-term strategy to an ongoing market for family member's stock.

Cons: Subjects the business to expectations among most private investors of higher total returns than either lenders or public stockholders. Poses other potentially restrictive terms: Private partners may ask to take control of the business if certain targets are not met; they may require options obligating the company to buy them out by a certain time; they may require anti-dilution provisions that restrict issues of new stock. Also, raises the risk that a financially strong partner may eventually be able to acquire a controlling interest in the company by gradually buying up family members' shares.

C2. Initial Public Offering of Subsidiary

Definition: This technique involves incorporating a division or operation of the company as a separate subsidiary, then selling stock in it to the public.

Purpose: Provides capital for a wide range of uses.

Pros: Allows access to public capital markets without taking the whole company public. Creates a new "acquisition currency" for the family in the form of a public stock that can be used to exchange for other assets or acquisitions.

Cons: May be difficult to separate a division or operation from the parent company. Can have negative tax implications. Requires offering of a unit that is large enough to go public — a threshold that has been rising in recent years. As in any public offering, entail significant fees and registration and disclosure requirements.

C3. Strategic Alliances and Joint Ventures

Definition: Long popular in Europe and Japan, joint ventures and strategic alliances are growing in North America too. These agreements allow two or more companies to pool resources to pursue a common strategy for mutual benefit. Prospective partners include any business entity, including other family businesses, with compatible industrial assets and complementary characteristics. Typically, joint ventures involve shared funding of a project, while strategic alliances, a closer kind of linkage, involve shared ownership of equity and resources associated with the project. An estimated 20,000 alliances were formed in the U.S. between 1987 and 1992, nearly four times as many as between 1980 and 1987.

Purpose: Enables the company to pursue opportunities that it would be unable to pursue alone.

Pros: Allows the company to build strengths in more business areas than the company is capable of developing alone. Provides access to capital at relatively low cost because both partners see synergies to be gained, including leveraging partners' differing capabilities, market knowledge, management skill and capital to the benefit of both. Eases access to outside management, assuming that the partners form a holding company that recruits outside managers for the project. If a family business partners with another family business, it can create what might be called an "External Family Effect," with both partners more likely than nonfamily businesses to share a certain "world view," including a commitment to long-term strategies, goals and values. In addition, the "Internal Family Effect" discussed earlier can increase the likelihood that shareholders of both partners will demand lower short-term returns in pursuit of shared long-term goals.

Cons: Requires careful planning, including a realistic feasibility study, analyses of business risk, careful budgeting, due diligence work and agreements to split rewards fairly based on risk and performance. Poses many potential pitfalls, including a failure of trust or communication; over-possessiveness by one partner; vague objective and goals and a failure to attract the best managers.

C4. Joint Venturing of Assets

Definition: This technique involves attracting outside investors to certain assets of the company, such as a piece of real estate or a marketing organization.

Purpose: To raise capital without diluting family control of the main business.

Pros: A highly flexible financing tool.

Cons: Can pose difficulties finding an outside partner who sees similar synergies and value in a particular joint venture. As in the case of all ventures that involve outside partners, risks opening the door to a financially strong entity that might eventually find a way to assume control.

C5. Syndicate Separate New Operations

Definition: This technique involves finding outside partners to provide capital to set up new branches, outlets or stores that will be operated by the family business.

Purpose: Provides capital for business expansion.

Pros: Leverages the capabilities of the business without assuming all the risk of new operations. Allows the family to maintain control of the business.

Cons: May be difficult to find syndication partners with the necessary financial strength, integrity and commitment. Must be structured carefully, attending to the same wide range of issues that arise with any outside equity investor.

VII. *Summary*

Financial management of the family business has entered a new era. In the past, business owners facing a capital or liquidity squeeze often felt they had very restricted choices once they ran out of debt capacity: limiting growth, selling out or going public. Today, business owners have many new, less drastic financial techniques at hand to weather financial transitions. Careful planning to meet capital and liquidity needs, often coupled with these techniques, can help the family business survive the many transitions in ownership, management and strategy that must be made if it is to endure through the generations.

Important principles and patterns lay the foundation for capital and liquidity planning. To sustain family control, the business owner must plan to manage some financial pressures innate to family businesses. The business' need for capital and shareholders' need for liquidity must by kept in equilibrium to avoid liquidity crises. This delicate balance is illustrated by the Family Business Triangle, which shows how family control can be lost if either capital or liquidity needs go unmanaged. Neglecting shareholder liquidity needs can cause a downward liquidity spiral that can weaken the business and ultimately leave shareholders little choice but to sell or liquidate it.

Another fundamental principle in managing capital and liquidity needs is to understand and manage your cost of capital. Cultivating shareholder unity and understanding of the business and its strategy is an important requirement for keeping capital costs low. Satisfied, confident shareholders tend not to demand high current returns on their equity because they believe in the business' long-term potential. This condition, which we have named the Family Effect, can significantly reduce the business' cost of capital and greatly increase its competitive advantage. Also, meeting shareholders' liquidity needs on a planned, sustainable basis can help keep them under control. If no liquidity is provided to shareholders, they are more likely to demand high current returns.

The perceived riskiness of the investment, the level of liquidity and the Family Effect are major components that help determine family business shareholders' expectations of the rate of return they must receive. This interplay is summarized in the Family Shareholder Return Formula. As the formula shows, cultivating the Family Effect and planning for shareholder liquidity are not peripheral activities. They are fundamental to sustaining the core competitive advantage of the family business: low-cost, patient capital.

Finally, this booklet describes twenty-two financial solutions that can help meet liquidity or capital needs. Some require outside capital and others do not. Some entail shifting from 100 percent family ownership of the business to family control of the business, and others do not. But all, under the right circumstances, can help the business owner's family maintain control over decisionmaking in order to make wise, well-timed choices about the future of the business and the family.

Index

57

The Authors

François M. de Visscher is president of Greenwich CT based de Visscher & Company. His firm is an independent financial advisory and investment banking concern that designs and implements financial solutions to the liquidity and capital needs of families in the business. He is the former managing director and founder of the family business group at Smith Barney, Harris Upham & Co. Inc. in New York, and has experience as an investment banker and an accountant. Mr. de Visscher also is actively involved in his own family business, a multibillion dollar steel wire manufacturer now in its fourth generation of family ownership. He also has served as president of the Family Firm Institute.

Craig E. Aronoff, Ph.D., holds the Dinos Eminent Scholar Chair of Private Enterprise and is professor of management at Kennesaw State University (Atlanta). He founded the university's Cox Family Enterprise Center. The center focuses on education and research for family businesses, and more than 100 universities worldwide have emulated its programs. In addition to his undergraduate degree from Northwestern University and Masters from the University of Pennsylvania, he holds a Ph.D. in organizational communication from the University of Texas.

John L. Ward, Ph.D. is Clinical Professor of Family Enterprises at Northwestern University's Kellogg Graduate School of Management. He is a regular visiting lecturer at two European business schools. He has also previously been associate dean of Loyola University Chicago's Graduate School of Business, and a senior associate with Strategic Planning Institute (PIMS) Program in Cambridge, Massachusetts. A graduate of Northwestern University (B.A. and Stanford Graduate School of Business (M.B.A. and Ph.D.), his Keeping the Family Business Healthy, Strategic Planning for the Family Business (authored with Randel S. Carlock), Creating Effective Boards for Private Enterprises are leading books in the family business field.

Together Dr. Aronoff and Dr. Ward are recognized as leaders in the family business field. Founding principals of The Family Business Consulting Group, they work with thousands of family businesses around the world. Recipients of the Family Firm Institute's Beckhard Award for outstanding contributions to family business practice, they have spoken to family business audiences on every continent. The books include Family Business Sourcebook II, the three volume series, The Future of Private Enterprise and the fifteen volume series, Family Business Leadership Series.

The best information resources for business-owning families and their advisors

The Family Business Leadership Series

Concise guides dealing with the most pressing challenges and significant opportunities confronting family businesses.

Comprehensive — Readable — Thoroughly Practical

- *Family Business Succession: The Final Test of Greatness*
- *Family Meetings: How to Build a Stronger Family and a Stronger Business*
- *Another Kind of Hero: Preparing Successors for Leadership*
- *How Families Work Together*
- *Family Business Compensation*
- *How to Choose & Use Advisors: Getting the Best Professional Family Business Advice*
- *Financing Transitions: Managing Capital and Liquidity in the Family Business*
- *Family Business Governance: Maximizing Family and Business Potential*
- *Preparing Your Family Business for Strategic Change*
- *Making Sibling Teams Work: The Next Generation*
- *Developing Family Business Policies: Your Guide to the Future*
- New guides on critical issues published every six to twelve months

The Family Business ADVISOR Monthly Newsletter

Family Business Sourcebook II

Edited by Drs. Aronoff and Ward with Dr. Joseph H. Astrachan, *Family Business Sourcebook II* contains the best thoughts, advice, experience and insights on the subject of family business. Virtually all of the best-known experts in the field are represented.

Now Available:
John Ward's Groundbreaking Family Business Classics
- *Keeping The Family Business Healthy*
- *Creating Effective Boards For Private Enterprises*

For more information:
Business Owner Resources, P.O. Box 4356, Marietta, GA 30061
Tel: 800-551-0633 or 770-425-6673

See reverse side for order form

ORDER FORM
Prepayment is required.

_____ copies, *Family Business Succession: The Final Test of Greatness*

_____ copies, *Family Meetings: How to Build a Stronger Family and a Stronger Business*

_____ copies, *Another Kind of Hero: Preparing Successors for Leadership*

_____ copies, *How Families Work Together*

_____ copies, *Family Business Compensation*

_____ copies, *How to Choose & Use Advisors: Getting the Best Professional Family Business Advice*

_____ copies, *Financing Transitions: Managing Capital and Liquidity in the Family Business*

_____ copies, *Family Business Governance: Maximizing Family and Business Potential*

_____ copies, *Preparing Your Family Business for Strategic Change*

_____ copies, *Making Sibling Teams Work: The Next Generation*

_____ copies, *Developing Family Business Policies: Your Guide to the Future*

_____ **Total** Leadership Series (Titles Above)

$_____ Cost (number of books x price - See chart at right)

$_____ $69.00 (each) *Family Business Sourcebook II*

$_____ $24.95 *Keeping The Family Business Healthy*

$_____ $39.95 *Creating Effective Boards For Private Enterprises*

$_____ **Subtotal**

$_____ $149.00* yearly, *The Family Business ADVISOR*

$_____ **Total**

$_____ Georgia residents add 6% sales tax to **Total**

$_____ Add 7% Shipping (10% Foreign) to **Subtotal**

$_____ **Grand Total** (US dollars only)

LEADERSHIP SERIES Multi-Volume Discounts *(Any title combination)*	
1 booklet:	$14.95
2 - 9:	$13.50 ea.
10 - 24:	$12.00 ea.
25 - 49:	$10.50 ea.
50 - 99:	$9.00 ea.
100+:	$7.50 ea.

*Add $15 - Canada and Mexico / $30 - All other countries.

Check enclosed_____ Credit card: MC_____ Visa _____ AMEX_____

Account No._____ Expires_____

Signature_____

_____ **Please enter my standing order for**_____ **copies of each future volume in The Family Business Leadership Series. I will receive a 20% discount from the list price on these volumes.**

SHIP TO: Name_____

Company_____Tel: (____) _____

Address_____

City_____ State_____ Zip_____

Country_____

Return this form to: Business Owner Resources; P.O. Box 4356; Marietta, Georgia 30061-4356

For fastest service, fax to 770-425-1776 or call 1-800-551-0633